green bean
celery
dill
potato
scallion

look and cook

FRESH

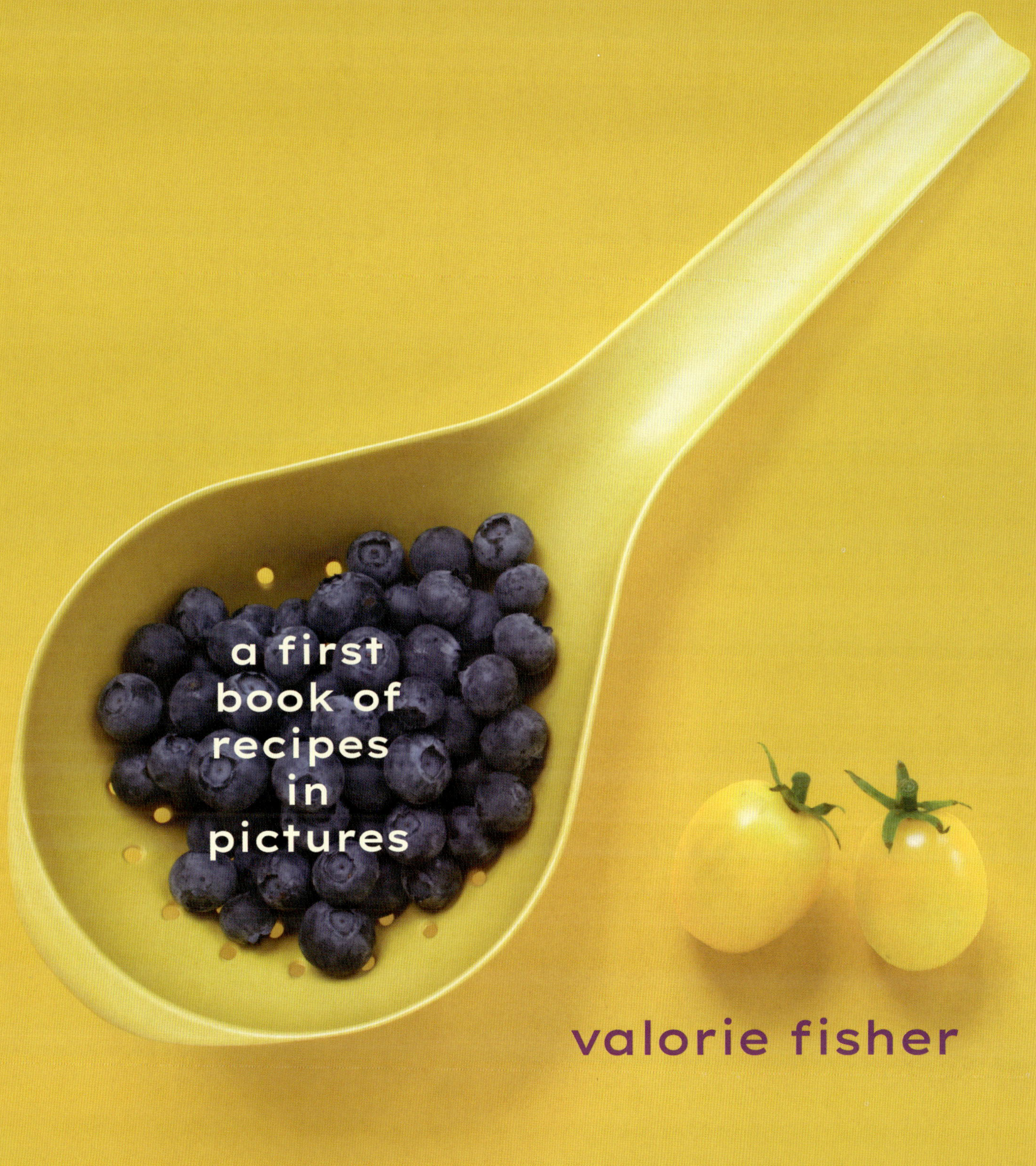

a first book of recipes in pictures

valorie fisher

ASTRA YOUNG READERS
AN IMPRINT OF ASTRA BOOKS FOR YOUNG READERS
New York

WHAT TO COOK

USING THIS BOOK

Look and Cook was created with young chefs in mind, those who might not yet be confident readers but are adventurous eaters and enthusiastic helpers in the kitchen. Through simple pictures, these visual recipes allow kids to understand and follow each step that goes into preparing a given food. This unique cookbook format encourages independence and means kids can take the lead in the kitchen, asking for assistance as they need it. Of course, we do recommend adults support kid chefs as they follow these recipes, especially in gathering ingredients and equipment beforehand and giving help whenever they see .

Kids will enjoy the process, the math, the mess, the magic, the cleanup (maybe), and, of course, sharing what they've created!

2 — Servings or amount the recipe makes

10 minutes — Time needed for the recipe or a step

Step supervised or done by a grown-up

IN THE KITCHEN

IN THE KITCHEN

GETTING STARTED

Read the recipe

Wash your hands

Wash all fruits and vegetables

Ask for help anytime you need it

Gather your kitchen tools

Gather your ingredients

Have fun

Help clean up

Mixing ingredients

Cracking an egg

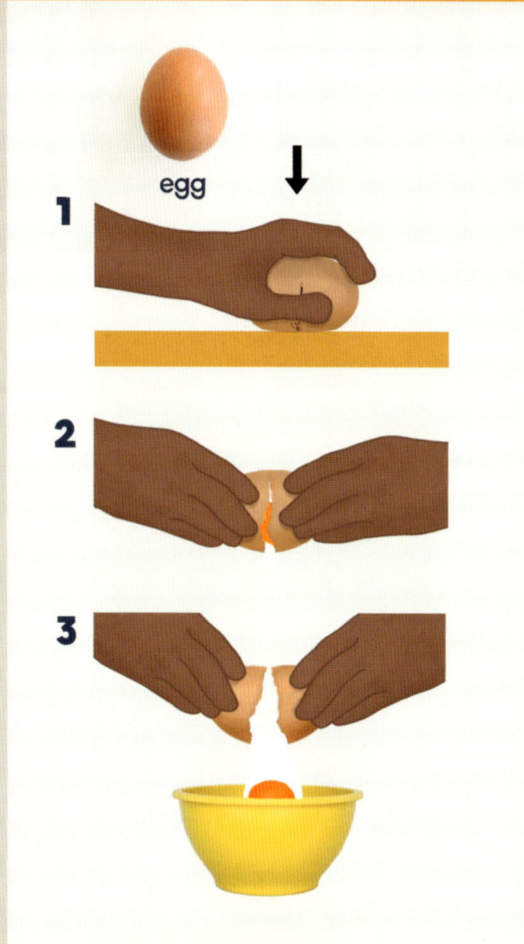

Measuring brown sugar

Opening ripe stone fruit

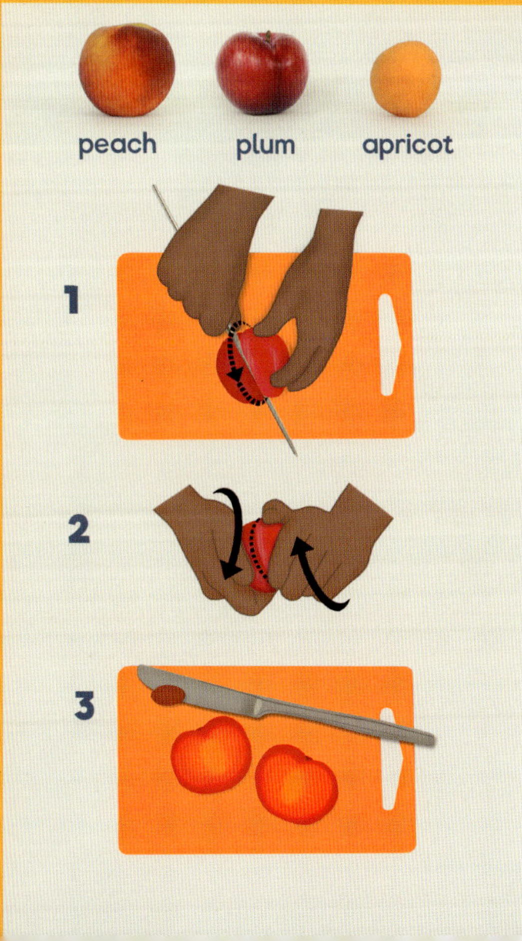

Juicing

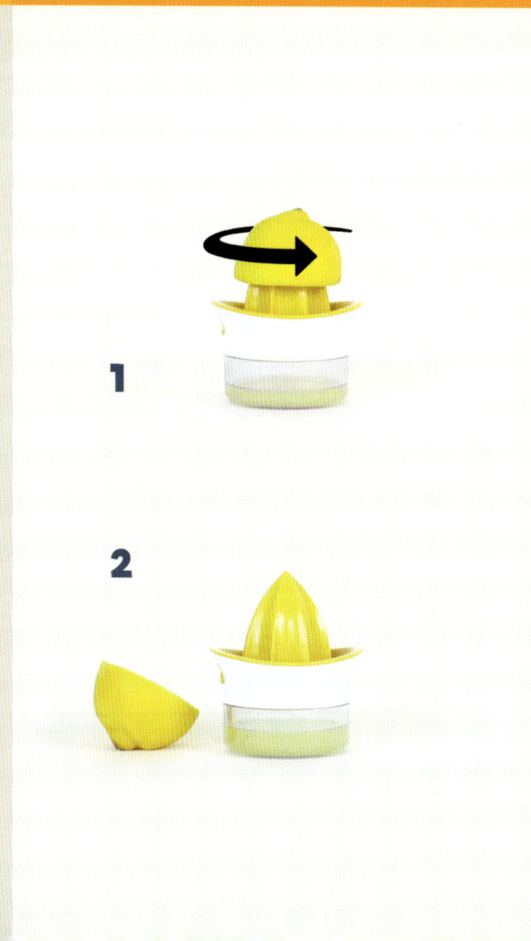

Baking toothpick test

Measuring butter

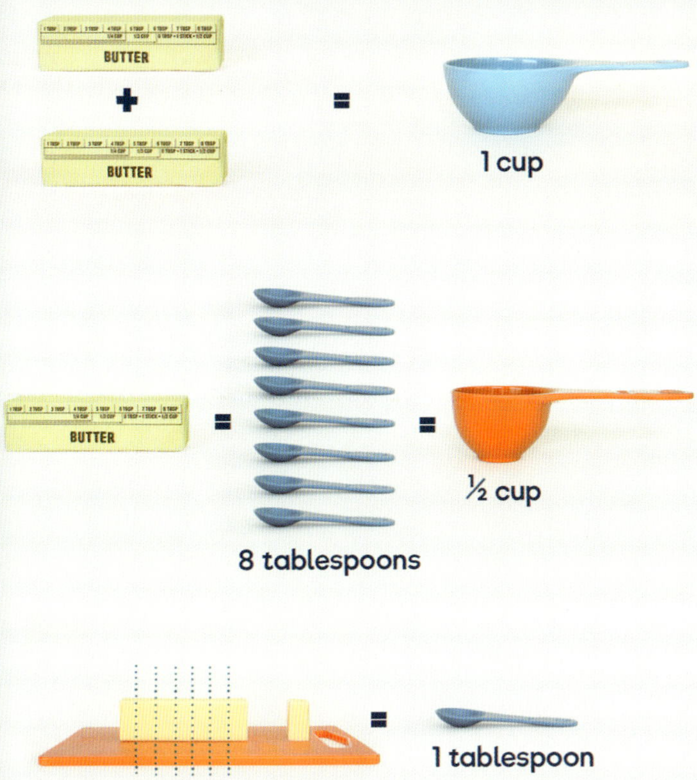

Measuring cups & spoons

Pressing garlic

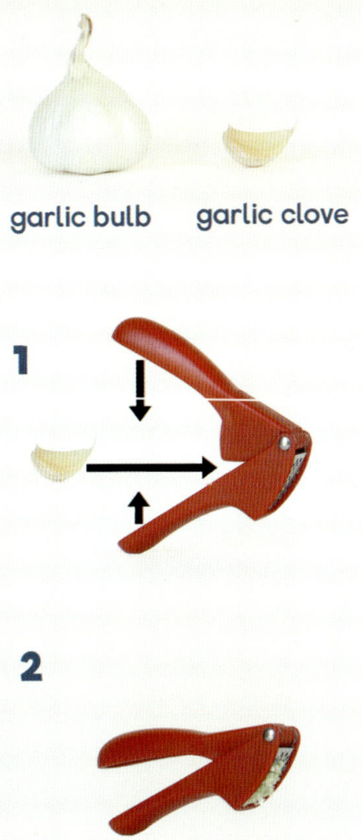

Pinch of salt

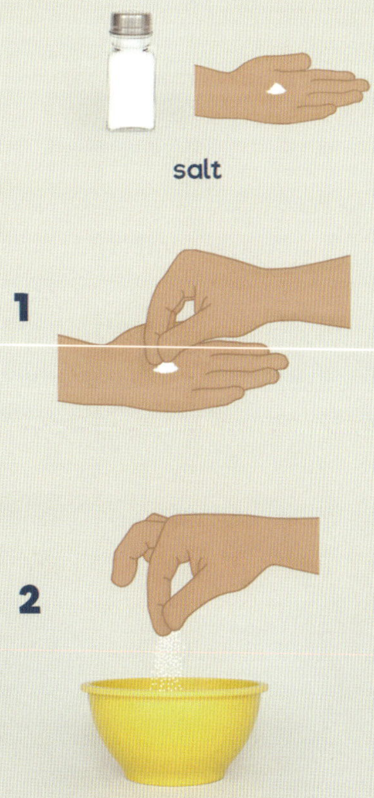

Snipping herbs

MINT MOXIE

4

15 minutes

1 cup
sliced strawberries

¼ cup honey

¼ cup lime juice

5 mint springs

water to fill jar

1 cup

sharp knife

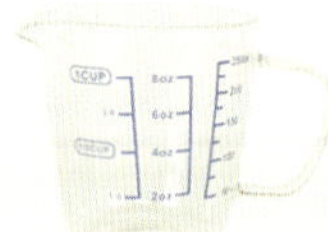

1 cup liquid measure

blunt knife

juicer

blunt scissors

string

mixing spoon

quart jar

small cutting board

1
2

2
1
2
3

3
1
2

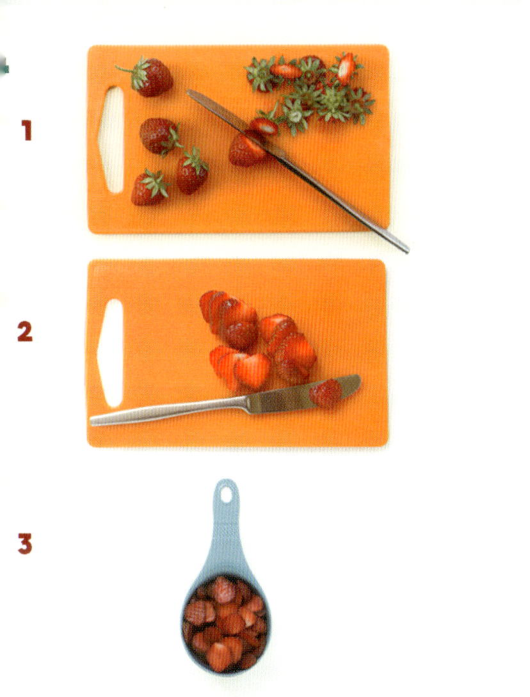
1
2
3

5
HONEY

6
1
2

8

9

SUNSHINE SALSA

- 3 cups cherry tomatoes
- ¼ cup cilantro leaves
- ¼ red onion
- juice of 1 lime
- 1 clove garlic
- ½ teaspoon of salt

- ½ teaspoon
- ¼ cup
- 1 cup
- garlic press
- juicer
- sharp knife
- small cutting board
- blender

QUICK KERNELS

1

10 minutes

ear of corn

pat of butter

pinch of salt

blunt knife

sharp knife

oven mitt

small cutting board

microwave

1

2

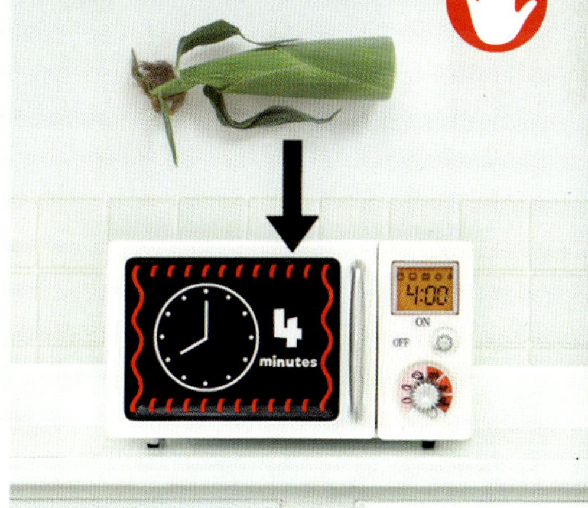

3

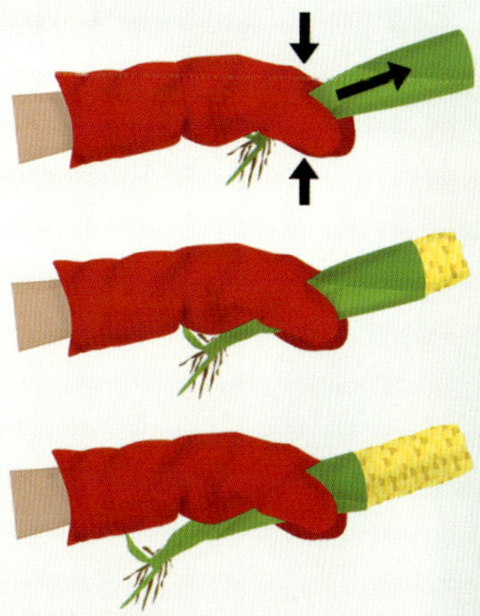

4

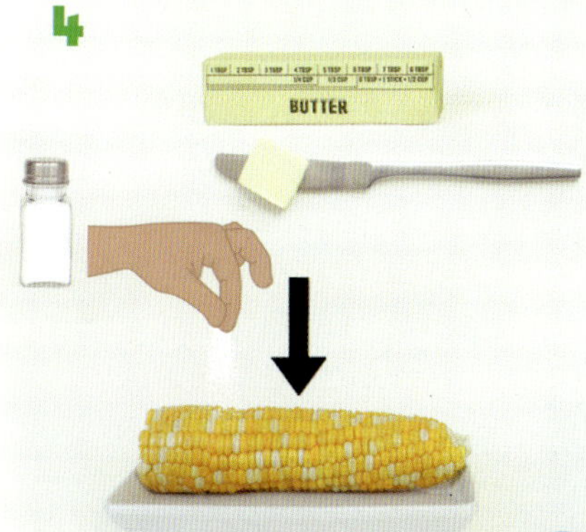

CORNFETTI

4

20 minutes

4 ears of corn

juice of 1 lime
½ teaspoon lime zest

1 tablespoon snipped chives

2 tablespoons cilantro

⅓ cup crumbled feta

1 tablespoon mayonnaise

¼ teaspoon salt

¼ teaspoon

½ teaspoon

1 tablespoon

⅓ cup

blunt scissors

mixing spoon

large bowl

juicer

large cutting board

oven mitt

sharp knife

microplane

microwave

1
2
6
minutes
6:00
ON
OFF
3
1
2
3
4
5
6
1
2
7
8
9
10
FETA
Mayonnaise
11
12

TWIGS

12

1 hour

1 sheet frozen puff pastry

1 egg

1 tablespoon water

⅓ cup shredded cheddar cheese

1 tablespoon snipped basil

1 tablespoon snipped parsley

1 tablespoon snipped chives

1 tablespoon

blunt knife

⅓ cup

fork

pastry brush

blunt scissors

rolling pin

small bowl

parchment paper

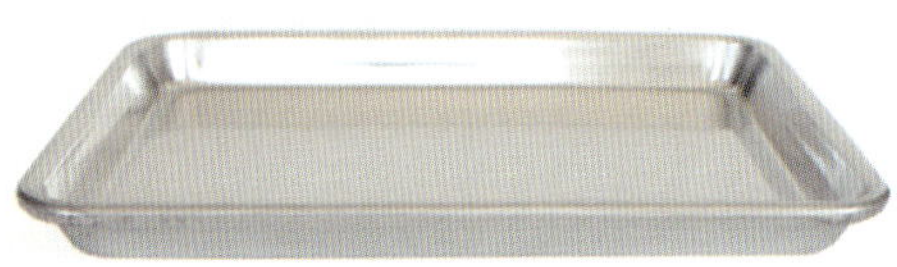

baking sheet

oven mitt

1
Puff Pastry Sheets
2 ready to bake sheets
30
minutes
2
375°F
3
nonstick, oven-safe
parchment paper
Puff Pastry Sheets
4
5
6
7
CHEDDAR
shredded cheese
8oz
8
9
1
= 12
2
10
11
22
minutes
12

CUMBER CURL

1

10 minutes

1 spinach tortilla | ½ cucumber | cream cheese | 6 mint leaves

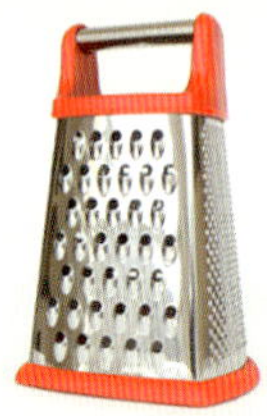

grater

blunt scissors

small bowl

blunt knife

large cutting board

CITRUS CIRCUS

6

15 minutes

- juice and zest of 1 orange
- juice of 1 lemon
- ⅓ cup olive oil
- 1 tablespoon honey
- 2 teaspoons yellow mustard

- 1 teaspoon
- juicer
- sharp knife
- 1 tablespoon
- microplane
- 1 cup liquid measure
- pint jar
- small cutting board

✱ **Use CITRUS CIRCUS with SPRING IN A JAR 18, or any salad.**

SPRING IN A JAR

1

10 minutes

3 sliced strawberries

1 tablespoon CITRUS CIRCUS 17

handful of baby spinach leaves

1 tablespoon sliced almonds

1 tablespoon

blunt knife

pint jar

small cutting board

1

2

3

4

Mix it up with different ingredients!

cherry tomato

lettuce

mini mozzarella balls

carrot

sprouts

radish

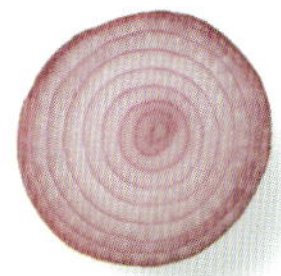
red onion

pomegranate

sunflower seeds

basil leaves

bell pepper

celery

apple

grapes

cucumber

pepitas

crumbled feta

chopped walnuts

avocado

mint leaves

SUMMER IN A SANDWICH

1

10 minutes

tomato

mayonnaise

pinch of salt

2 slices of bread

small cutting board

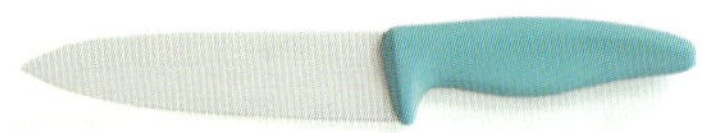

sharp knife

blunt knife

1

2

3

4

Follow steps 1, 2, and 3, then add additional ingredients on step 4.

1, 2, 3, 4 +

slice of fresh mozzarella

5 basil leaves

1, 2, 3, 4 +

slice of cheddar

lettuce leaf

1, 2, 3, 4 +

slice of avocado

bunch of sprouts

CARROT CRUNCH

4

20 minutes

3 cups
grated carrots

2 tablespoon
snipped mint

juice of
1 lemon

¼ cup
dried cranberries

2 tablespoons
olive oil

2 tablespoons
tahini

1 teaspoon
honey

¼ teaspoon
salt

¼ teaspoon

1 teaspoon

1 tablespoon

¼ cup

1 cup

blunt scissors

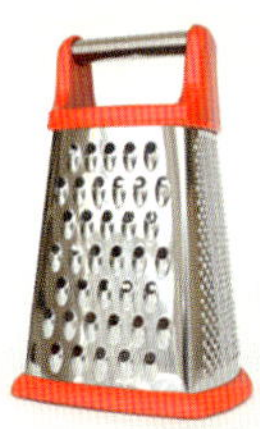

grater

sharp knife

mixing spoon

large bowl

juicer

large cutting board

1

1
2

2

3

4

OLIVE OIL
Tahini
ground sesame seeds
HONEY

5

6

7

dried sweetened CRANBERRIES

8

9

ZIPPERS

15-20

30 minutes

1 medium zucchini

⅓ cup shredded cheddar cheese

⅓ cup bread crumbs

½ teaspoon garlic salt

1 egg

1 tablespoon dill

✱ ZIPPERS are delicious with ZIP DIP **26** **!**

½ teaspoon

1 tablespoon

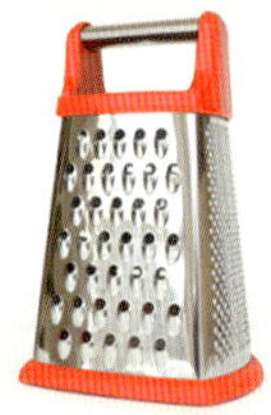

grater

⅓ cup

blunt scissors

spoon

kitchen towel

turner

2 small bowls

oven mitt

parchment paper

baking sheet

large cutting board

425°F
2
nonstick, oven-safe
parchment paper
3
1
2
5
6
GARLIC SALT
CHEDDAR
shredded cheese
8oz
Plain BREAD CRUMBS
8
9
1
2
11
15
minutes
12

ZIP DIP

6

10 minutes

½ cup plain Greek yogurt

1 teaspoon honey

¼ teaspoon garlic salt

1 tablespoon olive oil

1 tablespoon lemon juice

1 tablespoon snipped parsley

1 tablespoon snipped mint

¼ teaspoon

1 teaspoon

1 tablespoon

spoon

juicer

½ cup

small bowl

blunt scissors

small cutting board

1

2

3

4

5

6

PEANUT DUNK

5

15 minutes

½ cup peanut butter

2 tablespoons soy sauce

2 tablespoons rice vinegar

4 tablespoons water

1 teaspoon sesame oil

1 tablespoon maple syrup

1 teaspoon

spoon

small bowl

1 tablespoon

½ cup

1

2

3

4

STRAWBERRY SWAMP

3

40 minutes

2 cups sliced strawberries

2 tablespoons sugar

1 tablespoon

1 cup

spoon

small bowl

blunt knife

small cutting board

1

1

2

3

2

3

1

2

30 minutes

4

PINK DRINK

1

5 minutes

½ cup
STRAWBERRY SWAMP 28

1 cup milk

1 cup
liquid measure

blender

1

2

3

4

APPLE DROP

1

10 minutes

1 apple

1 tablespoon light brown sugar

2 pinches cinnamon

1 tablespoon dried cherries

pat of butter

1 tablespoon

blunt knife

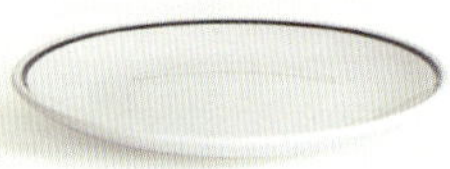

microwave-safe plate

sharp knife

microwave-safe bowl

small cutting board

microwave

2

3

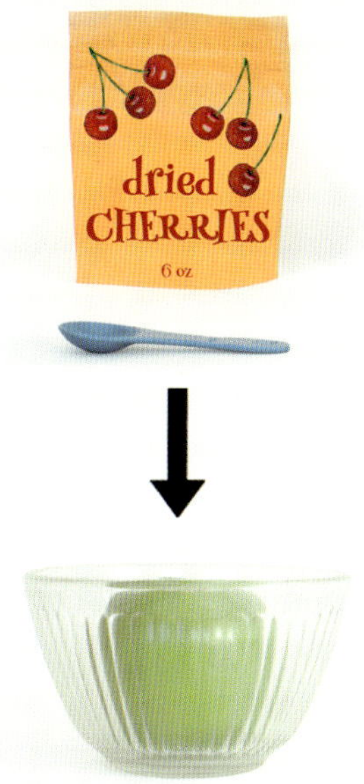
dried CHERRIES
6 oz

LIGHT BROWN SUGAR
1lb

5

CINNAMON

6

BUTTER

4 minutes
4:00
ON

8

5 minutes

9

CARROT CLOUD

9

50 minutes

1½ cup grated carrots

1¼ cup flour

1 cup light brown sugar

½ cup canola oil

2 eggs

1 teaspoon baking soda

1 teaspoon cinnamon

¼ cup chopped pecans

¼ cup raisins

✱ **Frost your CARROT CLOUD with CLOUD COVER 34!**

1 teaspoon

¼ cup

½ cup

1 cup

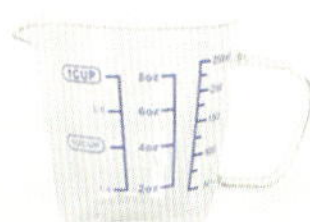

1 cup liquid measure

mixing spoon

large bowl

8"x 8" baking pan

spoon

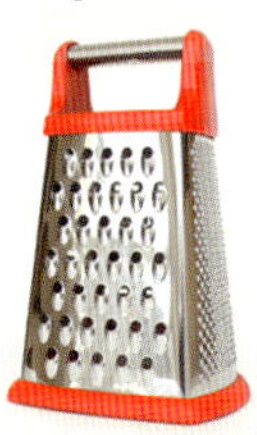

grater

parchment paper

large cutting board

toothpick

oven mitt

1
350°F
2
nonstick, oven-safe
parchment paper
1
2
3
1
2
+
4
LIGHT BROWN SUGAR
CANOLA OIL
5
FLOUR
CINNAMON
BAKING soda
+
6
7
chopped PECANS
Raisins
+
8
9
10
30 minutes
11
12

CLOUD COVER

9

35 minutes

8 oz package cream cheese

4 tablespoons butter

1 cup powdered sugar

1 teaspoon vanilla

1 teaspoon

mixing spoon

blunt knife

1 cup

large bowl

1

2

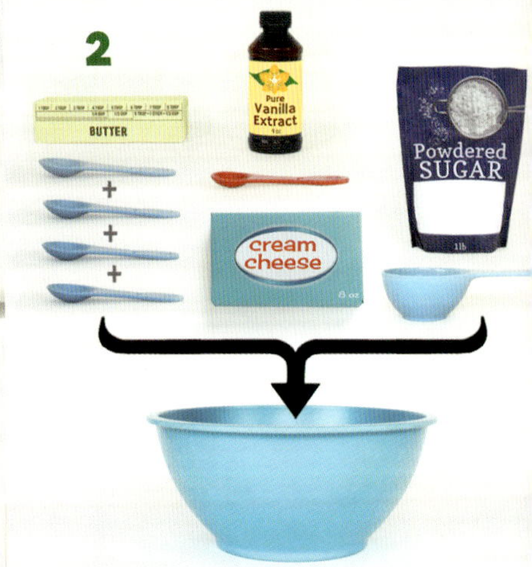

3

4

PURPLE SLURPLE

4

15 minutes

2 cups blueberries	juice of 2 lemons	⅓ cup honey	2 cups water

- ⅓ cup
- 1 cup
- 1 cup liquid measure
- juicer
- sharp knife
- small cutting board
- blender

HONEY BEARY

12

45 minutes

1¼ cup flour

¾ cup honey

1 cup raspberries

½ cup canola oil

1 egg

½ cup plain yogurt

2 teaspoons baking powder

1 teaspoon vanilla

1 teaspoon

¼ cup

½ cup

1 cup

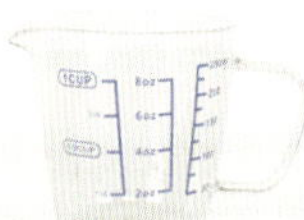

1 cup liquid measure

mixing spoon

large bowl

toothpick

12 baking cups

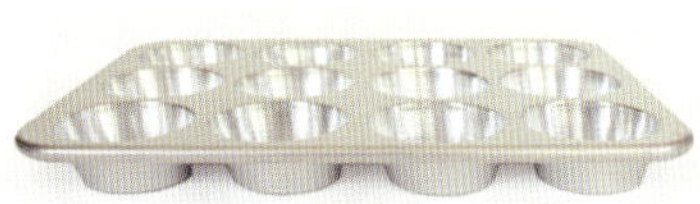

muffin tin

spoon

oven mitt

1

2

3

4

5

6

7

8

9

10

11

12

PEACH PARTY

4

15 minutes

4 scoops
vanilla ice cream

4 ripe peaches

1 cup
raspberries

2 tablespoons
sugar

1 tablespoon

spoon

1 cup

blunt knife

ice-cream scoop

fine sieve

microwave-safe bowl

small cutting board

small bowl

microwave

1

2

3

4

5

6

7

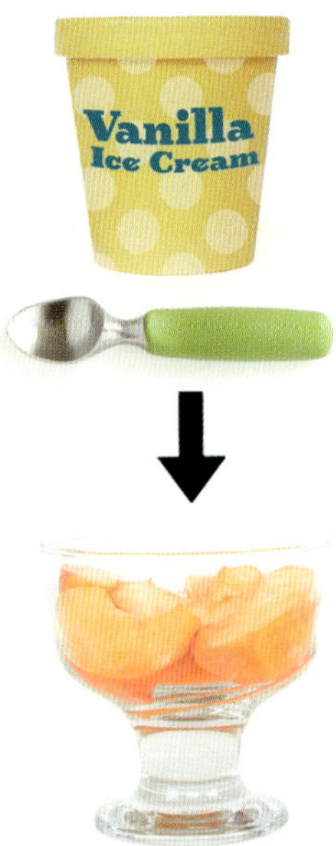

8

9

PLUMPIE

5

1 hour

1 plum

¼ teaspoon cinnamon

2 tablespoons sugar

1 egg

1 tablespoon water

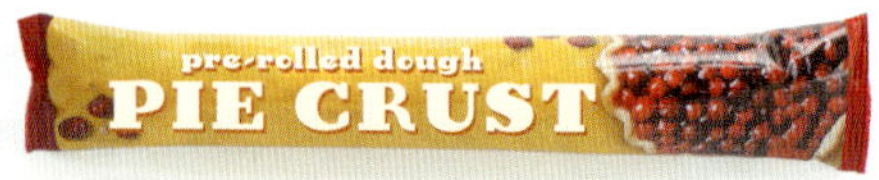

1 refrigerated pie crust dough

¼ teaspoon

fork

1 tablespoon

spoon

small bowl

blunt knife

5" round cutter

small bowl

oven mitt

pastry brush

parchment paper

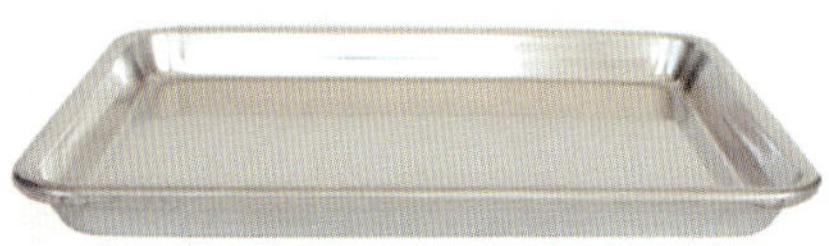

baking sheet

small cutting board

1
15
minutes
PIE CRUST
2
425°F
3
4
CINNAMON
SUGAR
5
pre-rolled dough
PIE CRUST
+
nonstick, oven-safe
parchment paper
6
1
2
7
8
1
2
9
0
SUGAR
11
15
minutes
12

Missing an ingredient? Substitute!

Mix it up! Switch out ingredients!

MIX IT UP!

HONEY
honey
Maple Syrup
maple syrup

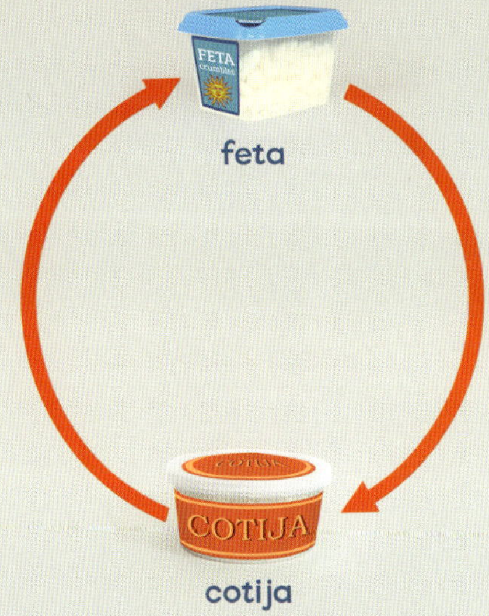
FETA
feta
COTIJA
cotija

dried sweetened CRANBERRIES
dried cranberries
Raisins
raisins
dried CHERRIES
dried cherries

sliced almonds
sliced almonds
chopped walnuts
chopped walnuts
chopped PECANS
chopped pecans

1 plum
1 peach sliced
OR
½ cup blueberries

For Mom and Dad for countless FRESH fun family meals. —VF

Copyright © 2026 by Valorie Fisher
All rights reserved. Copying or digitizing this book for storage, display, or distribution in any other medium is strictly prohibited.

For information about permission to reproduce selections from this book, please contact permissions@astrapublishinghouse.com.

Astra Young Readers
An imprint of Astra Books for Young Readers,
a division of Astra Publishing House
astrapublishinghouse.com
Printed in China

ISBN: 978-1-6626-2139-0 (hc)
ISBN: 978-1-6626-2140-6 (eBook)
Library of Congress Control Number: 2026934429

First edition

10 9 8 7 6 5 4 3 2 1

Design by Valorie Fisher
The text is set in Riffic Medium.
The titles are set in Riffic Bold.

Acknowledgments:
I am enormously grateful to Karen Hatt for her insight and keen eye. I would like to thank Jacque Schiller, Gina Maolucci, and Barbara Ensor for all their enthusiasm; Olive for her word jumbling skills; David and Aidan for their unflappable support; Susan Saccardi and Peter Busby for some peachy peaches; and Gunn Brook Farm Stand for delicious fresh vegetables. Last but not least, a huge thanks to my terrific team of young cooks, Hazel, Theodora, Molly, Nat, Cam, Oliver, Ellis, Grayson, and Genevieve.

About the art in this book:
A photographer, set designer, and adventurous home cook, Valorie Fisher combined all of these skillsets to create the photo illustrations in this book. Valorie constructs miniature sets incorporating kitchen tools, dollhouse miniatures, fruits, vegetables, and other ingredients, and then takes a picture.

bell pepper
parsley
parsley
pea
jalapeno
onion
cherry tomato